MAKE IT WITH
BURLAP

RUSTIC CHIC HOME DÉCOR AND MORE

Cheyanne Valencia

DESIGN ORIGINALS
an Imprint of Fox Chapel Publishing
www.d-originals.com

TABLE OF CONTENTS

Burlap is a versatile, eco-friendly, and economical fabric that you can use to make many fun and beautiful crafts.

Create looks ranging from rustic to elegant with this natural fabric. There are so many possibilities for home décor—you can make memo boards, table runners, throw pillows, napkin rings, and more. Let your imagination go wild by pairing all types of burlap with pearls, lace, beads, paint, wood, ribbon, feathers, and fabric to create one-of-a-kind items for your home and your life. Burlap has also become immensely popular for wedding and party decorating. Give burlap items as gifts, decorate with them for holidays, and even wear them as jewelry! Glue, paint, sew, gather, fray, dye, and layer your burlap to create a whole host of interesting effects. Whatever you can dream, you can do with burlap.

Let's get crafting with burlap!

BURLAP BASICS

With the recent popularity of this versatile fabric, you can now purchase burlap off of the bolt in a variety of colors and prints. Precut sheets of 1–2 yd. (1–2m) are available in many craft stores. The width is generally 45"–48" (115–122cm), but some are as wide as 60" (150cm). Burlap also comes in an array of precut ribbon widths with finished edges, frayed edges, or wired edges. You can even buy laminated burlap in 12" x 47" (30 x 120cm) rolls or by the yard in widths up to 60" (150cm).

There are generally two kinds of burlap weave. You can choose an open weave or close weave depending on what will work best with your project, or mix and match the weaves for added dimension. An open weave creates a rustic look. Light and billowy, it works well for projects like drapery, bows, and tablecloths. A close weave has a more refined look and can be used for projects like stenciling, pillows, tote bags, table runners, and placemats. An open weave is softer, loosely woven, and drapes well. It also allows light to shine through it. A close weave is coarser and tightly woven. It works well for light filtering.

Burlap color choices range from natural, brown, black, white, and oyster to red, blue, green, yellow, orange, and purple, and they also come printed with patterns like polka dots and chevrons. There is a rainbow of colors available; more will probably show up in stores by the time you read this book. If you can't find the exact color you're looking for, use fabric dye on white burlap to create just the right shade for a unique project. Follow the manufacturer's directions for dyeing and hang the burlap up to dry. If you plan on putting dyed burlap in the clothes dryer, expect it to fray quite a bit. Try sewing a zigzag stitch around the outer edges before dyeing the fabric.

Tip!
The projects in this book do not require the burlap to be pre-washed. If you are planning to wash your burlap, do your research carefully first. Washing burlap in a top-load washing machine can damage the machine due to fraying fibers.

TIPS AND TECHNIQUES

Burlap is easy to work with, but there are plenty of little tips and tricks that will make your life easier and make your projects come together in a jiffy. Take a look through the advice and techniques in this section before getting started to become a deft hand at manipulating burlap.

HOW TO CUT BURLAP

To cut burlap cleanly, evenly, and painlessly, remove one strand of jute to form a guideline and clear the way for the cut.

1 MEASURE TO THE CUT. Measure from the edge of the burlap to the point where you want to cut, and pull on one strand of the jute. You can use the tip of a heavy needle to get the strand started. This is most easily done along the fold in a large piece of burlap. It can also be done anywhere along the raw edge.

2 REMOVE THE STRAND. Pull the strand of jute, gathering the burlap, until you've completely removed the strand.

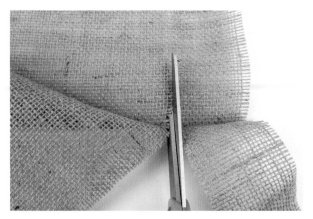

3 SEE THE GUIDELINE. Removing the strand of jute will leave a subtle, but clear, guideline to cut along. The guideline is even clearer when the burlap is not folded.

4 MAKE THE CUT. Cut through one layer at a time along the guideline.

How to Make Burlap Rosettes

Burlap rosettes are easy, fun, and used in so many different projects.

1 PREPARE THE STRIP. Cut burlap strips according to the project instructions; for example, the Grapevine Wreath project on page 20 uses strips that are 2" x 12" (5 x 30cm) and 2" x 24" (5 x 61cm). Begin to roll the end of one strip, using a small amount of hot glue to secure it in place. This will form the center of the rosette.

2 START THE ROSETTE. Hold the center of the rosette on one end and twist the strip away from you. Turn the rosette about a quarter turn to wrap the twisted strip around the center of the rosette. Hot glue into place between the layers where the glue will not be visible.

3 CONTINUE FOLDING. Continue to twist the strip and turn the rosette, gluing as you go.

4 FINISH THE ROSETTE. Secure the end of the strip on the back of the rosette, out of sight. You can trim away the rolled burlap stem on the back to make the rosette lay flat.

Tip! In this book, ribbon and fabric rosettes are made following these same instructions. However, the ribbon and fabric strips are first folded in half lengthwise before starting to roll the end. The folded edge should be used as the top edge of the rosette.

USING HEAT BOND TAPE

Many of the projects in this book use heat bond tape to fuse burlap together, which makes assembling the projects a cinch. These basic instructions apply in all cases, but you should also check the manufacturer's instructions before starting. Use a slip sheet to protect your ironing surface when using the tape. To use it, iron strips of the tape onto the burlap where directed. When you're ready to fuse, remove the paper backing from the tape. Then fold or place the burlap as directed and simply press firmly to create the bond.

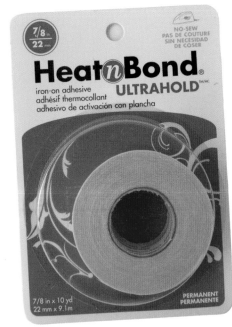

FRAYING AND GATHERING BURLAP

Some of the projects in this book require the burlap to be frayed and/or gathered. Here are some tips for those techniques.

FRAYING

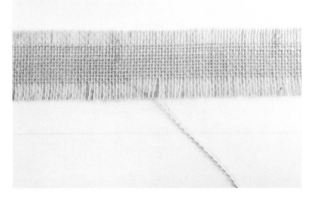

When fraying burlap, pull one strand of jute at a time until it's completely removed. The first few strands will come off very easily and you may be able to remove them two at a time. However, once the first few strands are removed, one at a time will work best.

Hold the burlap down close to the area where you're removing the jute strand for ease of removal and to minimize tangling of the frayed strands.

 Tip! Save extra pieces of jute to use as ties later.

GATHERING

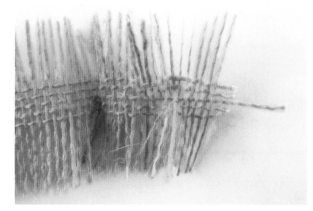

Decide which strand of jute you want to pull for gathering and pinch it between your thumb and forefinger. Use your other thumb and forefinger to grasp the strip of burlap and slide it down along the gathering strand.

The burlap strip will begin to look like this. It may begin to twist, but this just adds dimension, so let it twist naturally.

This is what a strip of burlap gathered from both ends looks like.

Tip! Do all of your burlap gluing on top of wax paper so that you don't get glue all over your table! Some glue always goes right through the burlap weave, no matter how careful you are.

MATERIALS

You may already have many of the craft supplies used in this book on hand. Along with some basic must-have materials, there are a lot of supplies out there that can be used to embellish burlap. Feature your favorite colors, textures, and items to make each project your own!

Adhesive labels

Ribbon

Fabric

Craft paint

Gift bags

Beads and buttons

Feathers

Craft rope/
twine

Paper and fabric doilies

Natural accents

RECOLLECTIONS™
Craft It™ | Cruez-le | A Crear Artesan.
Rope | Corde
Cuerda

15 yd / 13.7 m

0.1 in / 3 mm

Cork

Glue

4 fl OZ (118 mL)

Cardstock/
patterned paper

BURLAP WREATH

This classic burlap project comes together in a matter of moments! You'll need a lot of burlap to make a nice, full wreath, but once you have the finished wreath in your hands, you'll know it's worth it.

MATERIALS

12" (30cm) wire wreath frame • 34–37 ft. (10–11m) of 5–6" (12–15cm)-wide burlap garland • Wire or pipe cleaner (optional) • Accent color burlap • Hot glue

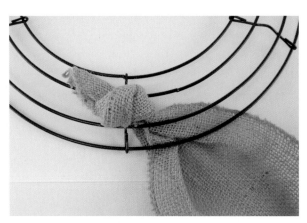

1 TIE ON THE BURLAP. Knot the end of the burlap garland to the wire frame, or attach it with a small piece of wire or pipe cleaner.

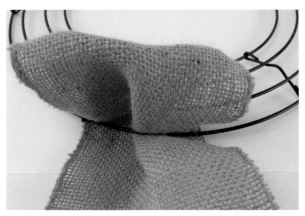

2 MAKE THE FIRST PUFF. Push a 5"–6" (12–15cm) loop of burlap up through the back of the outer ring.

3 MAKE THE NEXT PUFFS. Holding the first puff of burlap in place, push up two more loops of the same size to make two more puffs, first going up through the middle ring and then going up through the inner ring. You should end up with three even puffs.

4 CONTINUE THE WREATH. Scrunch these puffs all to one side and then begin again on the outer ring. You can twist the burlap strip once before beginning again if it helps. Repeat the loops up to three times within each divided section of the wire wreath. When you're done, decorate the wreath with rosettes attached with hot glue.

Tip! The wreath shown here used about 37 ft. (11m) of garland, and the finished wreath is approximately 17" (43cm) wide. Make this wreath with less garland by making smaller loops or making two sets of loops per section instead of three.

GIFT BAG

Tired of giving gifts in the same old store-bought gift bags? Create a customized carrier for your gift instead using some basic burlap and some elegant beads. It's like a bonus gift in and of itself!

MATERIALS

Medium-size paper gift bag (8" x 4.75" x 10" [20 x 12 x 25cm]) • 6½" (16cm)-diameter paper doily • Six ½" (1cm) pearl beads • Burlap strips in mixed colors: two 2" x 8" (5 x 20cm); two 2" x 10" (5 x 25cm); two 2" x 12" (5 x 30cm) • Spray adhesive • Hot glue

1 ATTACH THE DOILY. Spray the back of the paper doily with adhesive and apply it to the front of the gift bag.

2 GATHER THE BURLAP. Pull the center jute strand on each end of each strip and gather the burlap in the center. Since you want to gather the burlap from both ends, secure one end of the strand and start gathering at the other end. Then switch ends to finish gathering toward the middle.

3 TIE OFF THE BURLAP. Gather each strip as tightly as possible and tie the strand ends together in a knot, creating a sort of burlap pouf. Trim the ends of the strands very short.

4 FINISH THE POUFS. Pull and remove some of the jute strands along the outer gathered edges of the poufs to fray the burlap. Use hot glue to attach the poufs to the doily. Glue pearl beads in the center of each pouf.

Tip! Make a burlap gift tag for each gift bag out of a piece of cardstock and a burlap scrap.

FRINGE VASE

This tall vase has a touch of the groovy about it—especially if you choose to use colorful burlap—but it's mostly just a solid rustic piece to feature in a living room, kitchen, or dining room. Fill it with flowers to keep it classic or feathers to make a fresh statement.

MATERIALS

Tall 6" x 12" (15 x 30cm) French bucket vase • 144" (370cm) of 2" (5cm)-wide strips of burlap • Hot glue • 5 yd. (5m) of 1½" (4cm)-wide fabric ribbon

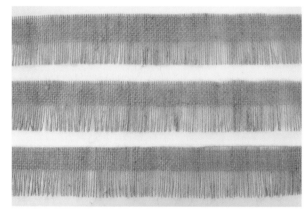

1 FRAY THE STRIPS. If using burlap yardage, cut the burlap in 2" (5cm) strips across the width (selvage to selvage) of the fabric. Pull and remove some jute strands along one long edge to fray the burlap about 1" (2.5cm) deep (about 10 or 11 strands). Save three or four strands for later.

2 GLUE THE STRIPS TO THE BUCKET. Using hot glue, attach the burlap to the back of the vase approximately ¼" (0.5cm) from the bottom. Continue gluing and turning the bucket, overlapping the layers as you move upward.

3 CONTINUE GLUING THE STRIPS. When one strip ends, glue its end securely to the bucket, and then begin gluing the next strip, matching up the fringe and weave as closely as possible.

4 DECORATE THE VASE. Create about fourteen rosettes from the fabric ribbon using 12" (30cm) strips (steps on page 9). Use hot glue to attach the rosettes to the vase. Finish the vase with a few of the jute strands pulled from the burlap tied into a bow and tacked in place with hot glue around the rim.

GRAPEVINE WREATH

The wreath base for this project is perfectly matched to the rustic look of the burlap flowers that adorn it. Here is just one application of the burlap rosette technique.

MATERIALS

Large grapevine wreath • Burlap strips in coordinating colors: eight 2" x 24" (5 x 61cm); eight 2" x 12" (5 x 30cm) • Hot glue • Small piece of wire for hanging • 1½ yd. (1.5m) of 1½" (4cm)-wide fabric ribbon (optional)

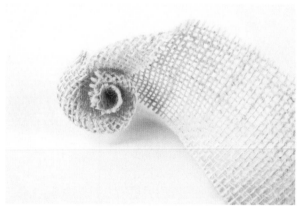

1 MAKE THE ROSETTES. Cut about 16 total strips of burlap for large and small rosettes as described in the materials list. Make the strips into rosettes (steps on page 9).

2 ARRANGE THE ROSETTES. Place all of the rosettes on top of the wreath to decide on the arrangement you'd like. Then remove them and put them aside in the same order so you can glue them onto the wreath quickly and accurately.

3 START GLUING. Using hot glue, begin gluing the rosettes onto the wreath, starting from the center point of your arrangement.

4 FINISH GLUING. Continue adding rosettes until you've finished the arrangement. Attach a small wire loop on the back of the wreath for hanging. If desired, loop a length of fabric ribbon around one of the vines and tie it into a bow for decoration.

PLACEMAT AND SILVERWARE HOLDER

Burlap table settings make a great backdrop for a fresh, home-cooked meal, no matter what your favorite dishes are. The patterned fabric ruffles and ribbon make a nice complement to the texture of the burlap.

MATERIALS

Burlap rectangles: one 14" x 20" (35 x 51cm) and one 5" x 15" (12 x 38cm) • 1" (2.5cm)-wide heat bond tape • Cotton calico fabric strips: two 3" x 36" (7.5 x 91cm) and one 1¼" x 36" (3 x 91cm) • Straight pins • Sewing needle and thread

1 START THE PLACEMAT. On the large burlap rectangle, remove one strand of jute 1" (2.5cm) in from every edge to create a border line. Follow the lines to cut 1" (2.5cm) squares from each corner. Cut four pieces of heat bond tape and attach them along the four edges. Fold the edges over and press to bond (technique on page 10).

2 MAKE THE RUFFLES. Fold the short end of one of the long fabric strips ¼" (0.5cm), then fold again. Use a needle and doubled thread to start a gathering stitch about ¼" (0.5cm) in from one long edge. Stitch across the length of the strip, folding the other short end under by ¼" (0.5cm) twice. Gather the ruffle to 12" (30cm) and knot the thread. Repeat with the other fabric strip.

3 SEW ON THE RUFFLES. Spread the ruffles evenly across the 12" (30cm) gathering thread. Pin the ruffles to the short ends of the placemat at ½" (1cm) from the edge and stitch them in place.

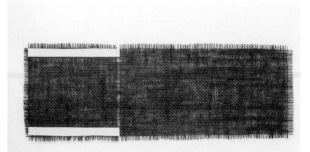

4 MAKE THE UTENSIL HOLDER. Prepare the small burlap piece as shown with the bottom 5" (12cm) ready for heat bonding, then fold the bottom up and press to bond. Use the heat bond tape to adhere the remaining strip of calico fabric to the silverware pocket.

Tip! Rip the fabric strips instead of cutting them by making a snip with the scissors and then ripping the fabric along the grain.

TABLE RUNNER

This piece makes a real statement! It's a great way to use up the pretty doilies you never quite had a use for. Let your inner artist emerge as you arrange the doilies in whatever creative pattern you envision.

MATERIALS

2 yd. (2m) or more of burlap (close weave is best) • Lace doilies in varying sizes and styles • Fray block • Straight pins • Sewing needle and thread

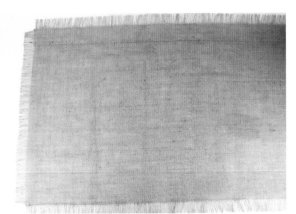

1 CUT THE RUNNER. Cut the burlap to the desired size. This table runner is 72" x 27" (183 x 69cm), including the fringe. Carefully remove some strands of jute on each edge to fray the fabric 1½" (4cm) deep (about 15 strands per edge).

2 PROTECT THE EDGES. At each corner, tie the two corner strands (one going in each direction) together into a knot to keep the fabric from fraying further. You can also use fray block around all the edges.

3 ARRANGE THE DOILIES. Arrange the doilies into the desired pattern. Start with the center doily first and work your way out in either direction. You can layer the doilies or choose to have them barely touching at the edges—whatever you like.

4 SEW THE DOILIES. Once you're pleased with the arrangement, use straight pins to hold the doilies in place. Then stitch them onto the burlap using a running stitch or a whipstitch.

Tip! Soak vintage doilies in very hot water with an oxygen cleaning detergent to return them to their original color. Hang them to dry and then press them with a hot steam iron.

RING BEARER'S PILLOW

Just a few folds and some delicate decorations are all it takes to make this beautiful yet functional pillow for the next special wedding you attend. With the handy ribbon ties, you can be sure that the ring bearer, whatever his or her age, won't lose the rings!

MATERIALS

10" x 21½" (25 x 54cm) piece of burlap • 8"–9" (20–23cm)-diameter lace doily • ¼" (0.5cm) pearl beads • 1½ yd. (1.5m) of ¼" (0.5cm)-wide ivory ribbon • 1 large button • ½" (1cm)-wide heat bond tape • Polyfil stuffing • Straight pins • Sewing needle and thread

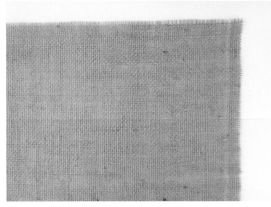

1 FOLD ONE EDGE. Remove one jute strand along one 10" (25cm) side of the burlap ½" (1cm) from the edge to create a fold line. Apply heat bond tape to the wrong side of the burlap between the edge and the fold line. Fold and press to bond (technique on page 10). Turn the burlap right side up.

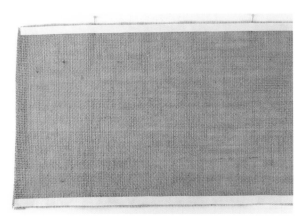

2 FOLD THE SIDES. From the folded edge, measure 4½" and 13½" (11.5 and 34cm); mark with pins to indicate the fold lines. Apply heat bond strips along both long edges of the burlap. Fold the burlap toward the center at the 4½" (11.5cm) mark and press to bond. Then fold the other side toward the center at the 13½" (34cm) mark and press.

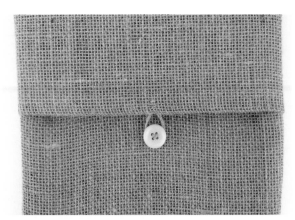

3 ADD A BUTTON. Turn the pillow case right side out and press. Sew on the button near the opening on the back of the pillow. Sew a piece of jute into a loop on the back of the pillow to slip around the button.

4 DECORATE THE PILLOW. Sew the doily to the front of the pillow. Embellish the doily with pearl beads. Finish the pillow with two small ribbon bows in the center. Be sure to attach the bows securely so the ribbons do not untie when attaching wedding bands. When finished decorating, stuff the pillow.

Tip! For a no-sew option, the doily can also be attached with heat bond tape, hot glue, or fabric glue, and the pearl beads can be attached with hot glue. Put a piece of wax paper inside the pillowcase when using glue of any type to protect the back of the pillow.

PEACOCK BOUTONNIERE

Whether you're preparing for prom, a wedding, or some other special event, you'll be sure to stand out with this unique and visually interesting accessory. If you need a different color scheme, simply experiment with a different kind of feather.

MATERIALS

Burlap squares: one 3" x 3" (7.5 x 7.5cm) and one 2½" x 2½" (6.5 x 6.5cm) • 2 peacock feathers • 2 peacock sword feathers • Fabric ribbon • Hot glue

1 MAKE THE BASE. With each burlap square, fold the two corners diagonally opposite one another down and in to form a cone shape. Secure the cones with hot glue.

2 START GLUING THE PIECES. Position the burlap cones to create a base for the arrangement and glue the tips together. Place all of the feathers on top of the burlap to decide on the arrangement. Then, remove the feathers and start by gluing the first sword feather in place.

3 FINISH GLUING THE PIECES. Glue on the two peacock feathers at the base. Glue the second sword feather in place at the base. Once it's dry, bend it slightly to one side to create a curve, then glue it in place just below the feathers.

4 FINISH THE BOUTONNIERE. Wrap the stems in ribbon, gluing it in place as you wrap. Apply a small amount of hot glue to the front of the ribbon wrap, then quickly bend the sword feather on the left to curve it down to the right side, gently laying it on the hot glue. Don't press the feather into the hot glue! Hold it in place until the glue dries.

Tip! For a smaller arrangement, trim the peacock feathers just outside of the color rings around the eye of the feather.

WEDDING CONE

Ivory ribbon and pearly buttons are perfect for any wedding that wants to mix classic with rustic. Fill these wedding cones with favors or flowers—whatever you choose, they'll make a delightful decoration on tables, chairs, or doors.

MATERIALS

10" x 10" (25 x 25cm) piece of burlap • 30" (76cm) of 1½" (4cm)-wide ribbon • Fourteen ⁷⁄₁₆" (0.5cm) buttons • 3 yd. (3m) of ¼" (0.5cm)-wide ribbon • Straight pins • Hot glue

1 CREATE THE CONE. Fold one corner of the burlap about three quarters of the way across diagonally and pin it in place. Apply hot glue along the edge of the folded corner. Fold the opposite corner over the hot glue. Remove the pins, apply hot glue along the underside edge of the second flap, and hold it in place until dry.

2 ADD THE HANGER. Flatten the cone and make a small cut on each side approximately 1" (2.5cm) from the top edge. Insert each end of the 30" (76cm) ribbon into the small cuts from the outside; tie each end into a loose knot inside the cone to hold it in place.

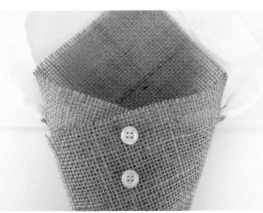

3 ADD THE BUTTONS. Cut the thin ribbon into eight 12" (30cm) strips. Then glue the buttons down the front of the cone, approximately ¾" (2cm) apart. Before gluing on the bottom button, fold one 12" (30cm) ribbon in half and glue the fold under the bottom button. Glue the remaining buttons around the top edge of the cone.

4 ADD THE RIBBONS. Tie the remaining ribbons into bows. Glue a bow in between each of the vertical buttons.

Tip!

To protect your work surface, work on top of wax paper when gluing the cone with hot glue.

THROW PILLOW

This puffy and fluffy pillow will jazz up any old sofa. You'll find yourself stroking the soft feather trim every time you sit down, and you're sure to get lots of compliments on your cool taste in décor as well.

MATERIALS

Two 11" x 19" (28 x 48cm) pieces of burlap • Two 11" x 19" (28 x 48cm) pieces of tan fabric (cotton or other) • 24" (61cm) braided trim • 2½ yd. (2.5m) feather boa • Polyfil stuffing • Three ½" (1cm) pearl beads • Sewing needle and thread • Straight pins • ½" (1cm)-wide heat bond tape

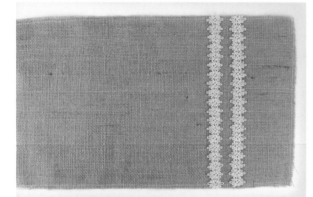

1 PREP THE PIECES. Pin each piece of tan fabric to the back of a burlap piece. Baste the edges at ¼" (0.5cm). Cut two pieces of braided trim to 11" (28cm) each and attach with heat bond tape (technique on page 10) to one of the burlap pieces vertically a few inches (centimeters) in from the right edge as shown.

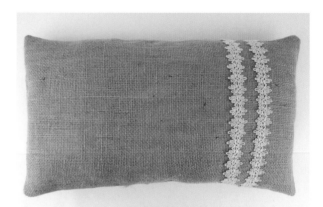

2 ASSEMBLE THE PILLOW. Place the two burlap pieces together with right sides facing and pin in place. Sew at ½" (1cm) around all sides, leaving an opening along the bottom edge for turning. Clip the corners and turn the pillow right side out. Stuff the pillow and stitch the opening closed.

3 ADD THE TRIM. Sew the feather boa to the edges of the pillow, tacking it about every 1½" (4cm). Start at the bottom center of the pillow.

4 EMBELLISH THE PILLOW. Use a 12"–18" (30–45cm) piece of feather boa to embellish the top left corner. Stitch one end in place at the center, then coil the boa around in a circle, tacking it down as you go. Tuck the end under and stitch it to secure it. Sew pearl beads in the center.

NAPKIN RINGS

Easy yet glamorous, these napkin rings add a serious boost of class to any dinner party. Don't forget the nice linen napkins to go with them!

MATERIALS

4" x 6½" (10 x 16.5cm) piece of burlap • 4" x 6½" (10 x 16.5cm) piece of transfer web • Hot glue • Freshwater pearl beads • Braided trim • Fray block • Sewing needle and thread (optional)

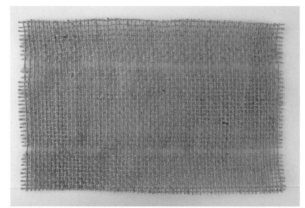

1 MAKE THE FOLD LINES. Remove a strand of jute from the long edges of the burlap 1" (2.5cm) in from each edge. These will be the fold lines.

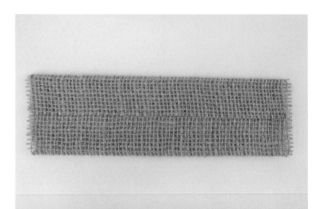

2 FOLD THE PIECE. Cut a piece (or pieces) of transfer web the size of the burlap piece. Adhere it to the burlap. Fold both long edges of the burlap in toward the center on the fold lines and press to bond. Trim the raw ends with scissors if necessary to square them up.

3 FORM THE RING. Apply hot glue across one short end of the strip. Bring the short ends together to form the napkin ring, overlapping the ends by ½" (1cm) and keeping the fold line to the inside. Press the ends together until the glue is dry.

4 EMBELLISH THE RING. Measure around the napkin ring before cutting the braided trim to size. Use fray block if needed on the ends of the trim. Hot glue the trim to the outer edges of the napkin ring. Attach pearl beads using either hot glue or by sewing them.

Tip! If you are sewing the pearl beads on instead of gluing them, it is easier to sew them down the center of the strip while it is still flat. Remember to leave ½" (1cm) on each end for the overlap.

GIFT-WRAPPED BOXES

These boxes work just as well as home and holiday decorations as they do actual gifts! Whether you give them away depends on how much you like what you come up with.

MATERIALS

9" x 9" x 4" (23 x 23 x 10cm) gift box • White gift wrap • Burlap strips: one 4"x 47" (10 x 119cm) and four 2" x 24" (5 x 61cm) • Mini pinecones • Jingle bells • Tape • Hot glue

1 START THE BOX. Wrap the box with white paper. Measure around the box and add 20" (50cm) to determine the length of the burlap strip. Cut a 4" (10cm)-wide strip of burlap to that length. Fray the edges. Tie the burlap around the box. Tie the strip once at the top of the box; don't make a knot until later.

2 GATHER THE BURLAP. Remove strands of jute one at a time from the long edges of each of the 24" (61cm) burlap strips until there are only about five strands left in the center of each strip. Pull the center strand of jute on each end and gather the fabric tightly in the middle of the center strand.

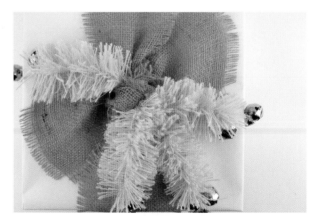

3 ADD BELLS. Tie jingle bells onto the gathering strand at one end. Space them apart and tie each one in place so it won't slide on the strand. Tie a knot after the last bell and trim the tail. Repeat this on all four gathered strips. Tie all four strips together with the bell-less ends into an "X" pattern. Leave the tails long.

4 DECORATE THE BOX. Lay the bell strips on top of the box. Use the tails to secure the bell strips to the burlap band, then trim the tails. Tie the burlap band into a knot around the bell strips. The ends of the band can be wrapped once more below the knot so they will lie flat on the box. Hot glue pinecones to the burlap decoration.

Tip! Use a variety of embellishments to adorn your gift boxes. Make the decoration a stand-alone piece, when possible, that can be tied on with the burlap band or attached with a safety pin. That way they can be easily removed when unwrapping the gift and can be reused on another occasion.

MEMO BOARD

A memo board should be big enough to handle everything you're juggling and pretty enough to merit all the space it takes up. This board certainly fits the bill with its colorful accents and multi-use face with both chalkboard and pinable surfaces.

MATERIALS

12" x 20" (30 x 51cm) decorative wooden plaque • 22" x 28" (56 x 71cm) stretched canvas • 22" x 28" (56 x 71cm) of cork tiles (or cork roll) • 28" x 34" (71 x 86cm) piece of burlap • Acrylic craft paint • Chalkboard paint • Mini paint roller • ½" (1cm) paintbrush • All-purpose glue • 56" (142cm) of 1½" (4cm)-wide ribbon • Staple gun

1 PAINT THE PLAQUE. Paint the edge of the wooden plaque with craft paint and allow it to dry. Apply chalkboard paint to the face of the plaque with a small paint roller, following the manufacturer's directions. Allow it to dry for 24 hours.

2 MAKE THE BOARD. Cut the cork tiles or roll to cover the stretched canvas surface and glue the cork in place using all-purpose glue.

3 COVER THE BOARD. Center the cork-covered canvas face down on the burlap. Wrap the edges of the burlap around the canvas to the back. Fold the edges of the burlap under by approximately 1" (2.5cm) before stapling them in place to the frame. Staple the top edge first, then the bottom, then the sides. Be sure to pull the burlap taut while stapling.

4 FINISH THE BOARD. Staple a 24" (61cm) length of ribbon to the top back of the frame for hanging, wrapping the ends of the ribbon under the lip of the frame. Staple a 16" (41cm) length of ribbon in each of the bottom corners of the memo board 3½" (9cm) from the corner in each direction. Glue the chalkboard in place as shown using all-purpose glue.

Tip! Measure for the placement of the chalkboard and mark the area with straight pins. Apply a generous amount of glue to the back of the chalkboard and the memo board surface, keeping the glue 1" (2.5cm) away from the edges.

WRIST CUFFS

Chunky bracelets like these beg to be noticed! Use your imagination
to create different decorated looks. Make bracelets in several colors to
match all your favorite outfits.

MATERIALS

4" x 10½" (10 x 27cm) piece of burlap • ¼" (0.5cm)-wide ribbon • 4" x 10½" (10 x 27cm) piece of transfer
web • Hot glue • Button • Decorative trim or lace • Large-eyed needle •
Sewing needle and thread

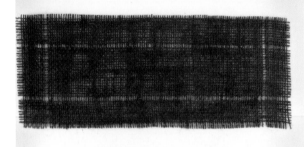

1 **MAKE THE FOLD LINES.** Remove a strand of jute
from all four edges of the burlap, 1" (2.5cm) in
from each edge. These will be the fold lines.

2 **FOLD THE PIECE.** Cut transfer web to the size of
the burlap piece. Adhere it to the burlap. Cut off
the corners of the burlap outside the fold lines. Fold
both long edges of the burlap in toward the center
on the fold lines and press to bond. Repeat with the
short edges.

3 **EMBELLISH THE EDGES.** Thread 1½ yd. (1.5m) of
ribbon onto a large-eyed needle and knot off
one end. Starting at the center point of one of the
short side edges, whip stitch around the entire cuff.
Make a button loop before knotting the ribbon. Sew
a button on the opposite end after checking for fit.

4 **EMBELLISH THE CUFF.** Decorate the cuff as desired.
This cuff is adorned with ribbon rosettes made
from 6" (15cm) lengths of ribbon (steps on page 9).
Use ribbons, lace, beads, or buttons to make a variety
of mix-and-match cuffs.

 If the cuff is too small for the intended wrist, increase the length to 11½" (29cm).

CURTAIN TIEBACK

Burlap makes a nice contrast to many typical curtain fabrics. Leave this
pull back simple with just the ribbon stitching, or decorate with rosettes
to match your curtains.

MATERIALS

11" x 30" (28 x 76cm) piece of burlap • 6 yd. (6m) of 1½" (4cm)-wide organza ribbon • Large-eyed
needle • 1" (2.5cm)-wide heat bond tape • Accent ribbon and fabric as desired for embellishments

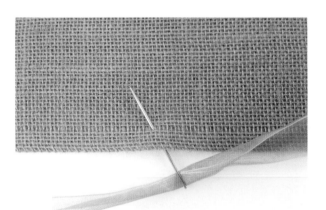

1 PREPARE THE BURLAP. Remove a strand of jute along
each long edge of the burlap at 3" and 3 ½" (7.5 and
9cm) and at 1" (2.5cm) from each short edge. Fold and
press at the 1" (2.5cm) lines toward the back, then do the
same on the 3" (7.5cm) lines. Use heat bond tape to fuse
the long edges together where they overlap on the
back (technique on page 10).

2 START THE STITCHING. Cut a piece of organza
ribbon 6 yd. (6m) long. Fit it through the eye of
the needle and knot one end. Starting at the center
of the burlap band, insert the needle up through the
back on the line where the jute strand was removed.

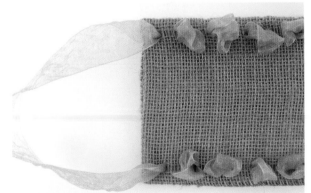

3 STITCH THE EDGES. Working clockwise, make
stitches about every ½" (1cm) using the line as a
guide. Pull almost all of the ribbon through on each
stitch, twisting it gently and leaving a bit of ribbon
puckered up before going on to the next stitch.

4 FINISH THE STITCHING. Stitch to one short end and
bring the needle out on top. Leave 9" (23cm) of
slack in the ribbon, then insert the needle in the top
of the opposite corner. Continue stitching until you
reach the starting point, making another loop at the
other end. Tie the ribbon into a knot on the back side
at the end of the last stitch. Embellish as desired.

The rosettes in this project are made from 3" (7.5cm)-wide cotton fabric strips folded in half lengthwise before rolling and cut in the following lengths: 12", 18", and 24" (30, 46, and 61cm) (steps on page 9). The burlap accent ribbon is 9" (23cm) long, tied into a soft knot. All of the embellishments are hot glued on.

Tip!

DECO BALLS

Deco balls can be used for any occasion and in any room. You can theme them for specific holidays or seasons, or just to match the color scheme of your living room. Try hanging them from houseplants or piling them artfully in bowls.

MATERIALS

4" (10cm) craft foam ball • 8" (20cm) twine • Five 1" x 36" (2.5 x 91cm) strips of burlap • Hot glue • 1½" (4cm) pearl head straight pins • Glass beads • Pearl beads • Ostrich feathers

1 ADD THE HANGER. Make a small hole in the top of the craft foam ball by pressing the hot tip of the glue gun into the ball for about four seconds. Fill the hole with glue and insert both ends of the twine.

2 COVER THE BALL. Glue the end of one of the burlap strips anywhere on the ball and begin to wrap it the way you would wrap a ball of yarn. Glue it periodically as needed. Continue, using all the strips, until the ball is completely covered.

3 DECORATE THE BALL. Use the pearl head pins to attach glass and pearl beads evenly spaced around the ball.

4 ADD FEATHERS. Before gluing the feathers in place, use the stem of the feather (or another pointed tool) to make a hole for each stem under the edges of the burlap. Fill the hole with glue and insert the feather until the stem disappears completely from sight.

Tip! You can find many different embellishments for these balls in the floral and jewelry departments of your local craft store. Make some for hanging and some without hangers to gather in a bowl.

Bonus Projects

Banner

This huge banner is actually a lot less work than it seems! Cut rectangles of burlap and fold them over the string to create each flag, gluing them together but not in place on the string. Spray paint wooden letters for the flags. Tie decorative strips of fabric and burlap between each flag.

Table Lamp

This delightful lamp was dyed and painted in a beautiful blue scheme. Dye white burlap to get just the right color, then make the fringe for the shade using the technique shown on page 18. Glue the fringe on in layers along with beaded ribbon. Finally, mask off the hardware and cord with painter's tape before spray painting the lamp.

COASTERS

These coasters are super easy to whip up! Make them using thick cork tile squares, frayed-edge burlap squares, felt squares, and ribbon. Using quick-dry tacky glue brushed on with a paintbrush, glue the burlap squares to the top of the cork tile and the felt square to the bottom of the cork tile. Decorate the coaster with a bit of ribbon and hot glue.

PLACE CARDS

Try making these adorable place cards for your next big event when you want to make sure tablemates are compatible! Just fold some decorative paper to create a stand-up card, and decorate the card with burlap and beads using hot glue. Add the names and you're done.

ABOUT THE AUTHOR

Cheyanne Valencia is the owner of Prairie Pony Mercantile in Bozeman, Montana. She has loved crafting since childhood when she first began stitching scraps of fabric together by hand. Coming from a long line of creative women, she is as equally talented with a glue gun as she is with a needle and thread. With a free spirit and an eclectic style, she roams the byways and small towns of Montana searching for inspiration in her creations. Her art ranges from simple and rustic to hip and modern. She makes unique crafts, often mixing old and new elements and styles. She sells her art at farmer's markets, craft fairs, quilt shows, festivals, and online. Cheyanne is also the co-author of *Sewing Pretty Bags: Boutique Designs to Stitch & Love* (Fox Chapel Publishing, 2015). To find out more about Cheyanne and her various creations, visit *prairiepony.com*.

PHOTO BY BRUCE LAURENCE JORDAN

ACKNOWLEDGMENTS

So many thanks to my big sister, designer Debra Valencia, for allowing me to ride her coattails into the world of professional crafting. I may now follow my dream of crafting and creating all day every day.
My thanks and gratitude to everyone at Fox Chapel Publishing for their support, guidance, and endless encouragement.